# HUMBLE MOMENTS

Part 1: I AM in the Stillness & the Chaos

THE CHRISTIAN NOMAD

# COPYRIGHT

# COLOPHON

IMAGES:
**Cover:** Filip Zrnzević La Plagne, Mâcot-la-Plagne, France
**Week 1:** Colin Rex - Grafarkirkja, Iceland
**Week 2:** Liam Simpson-Aoraki/Mount Cook National Park, New Zealand
**Week 3:** Samuel Scrimshaw
**Week 4:** Peter Winckler - Québec City, Canada
**Week 5:** Jared Rice - Yucatan, Mexico
**Week 6:** SweetIceCream Photography - Rivedoux-Plage, France
**Week 7:** Jenny Caywood - Brown house covered with snow
**Week 8:** Samuel Scrimshaw

All photos available on **Unsplash.com**

FONTS:
**Title Font:** Source Sans Pro (2012)
**Designer:** Paul Hunt
**Foundry:** Adobe Type

**Header Font:** Verdana (1996)
**Designer:** Matthew Carter
**Foundry:** Microsoft

**Body Font:** Arial (1982)
**Designers:** Robin Nicholas & Patricia Saunders
**Foundry:** Monotype Corporation

THE CHRISTIAN NOMAD **Font:** Grabriele Bad AH (2013)
**Designers:** Dave-Rakowski, Andreas Höfeld
**Foundry:** Fontgrube Media Design

# <u>DEDICATED TO</u>

*my loving and faithful wife.*
*we'll meet one day,*
*and it will be glorious!*


*Pastor John Stahl*
*who hugged me*
*when no one else*
*in the entire world would.*


*Chris White*
*who taught me*
*it's okay to question.*


*Dr. Mike Heiser*
*who showed me scripture*
*is the most amazing thing*
*in the entire world.*


*And Pastor Steven Furtick*
*who taught me*
*how to pray the scriptures*
*during one of the*
*darkest times of my life.*

# INTRODUCTION

This is not an exercise in wallowing in your own self-pity, this is written by a person that actually struggles with deep, deep depression and strong feelings of self-hatred. And it is being published and presented for people who also struggle with the deepest forms of depression. This is an exercise, for sure, but this is about allowing yourself to feel the emotions with which you are dealing and to allow them to breathe.

Thoughts are messy and unorganized. Plus they often make no sense. And frequently the only way to get them to make sense is by expressing them verbally. But other people don't understand your thoughts because they don't know why you are thinking them. You are the only one who can make sense of them. But most of the time you don't even know why you are thinking those thoughts, or what they actually mean. And worst yet are feelings, unfortunately, feelings are informed by your thoughts, so that explains why you can often neither understand them nor makes sense of them.

So what is the solution? Express them! Verbalize your thoughts!

But express them to the only two persons who can understand them and make sense of them: God and yourself. If you don't believe in God, then yourself and the wall. But just know, God is still listening, even if you aren't speaking to Him. Your emotions are real to you, even if they are not real to anyone else, even if they are not accurate or do not accurately reflect reality, they are still real. And you have to deal with them. So, get them out, you cannot shoo away a pest if the door or window is closed. And, how do you do that? By assessing your thoughts and allowing yourself to acknowledge your feelings and control them better so that each day you can become a better version of you.

And I hope this book helps  you in doing that.

- THE CHRISTIAN NOMAD

# HOW TO USE THIS

This is intended to be a short and quick version of the Lectio Divina to help one get closer to God through prayer and deep thought.

Each day should take no more than 3 to 5 minutes to complete.

I am developing this for myself, to help me get more consistent with my prayer time and focus my thought-life more on Jesus.

Like Lectio Divina this is to be done in 4 parts and reread each part 2 to 3 times each, before going to the next section:

Lectio = Read: Each day there will be a quote and a Scriptio = Scripture: read them several times slowly.

Meditatio = Meditate: Think about each word of the quote and consider all possible meanings and a deeper purpose.

Oratio = Pray: Pray the Scriptio, say it back to God as a statement of fact!

Contemplatio = Contemplate: Give at least 30 seconds considering your prayer on a deeper level and waiting on the Holy Spirit.

Whether you think you heard from God or not, go over the quote and Scriptio a final time and finish it off with an amen.

Then go about your day.

(maybe you will hear from God through another person)

# HOW TO USE THIS

Example:
**Lectio:** "It was a daring prayer offered by Augustine when he said "Lord hast Thou declared that no man shall see Thy face and live?--Then let me die, That I may see Thee." -Stanford
(Think about each word while rereading)

**Scriptio:** Isaiah 6:4-5 "And the posts of the door moved at the voice of him that cried, and the house was filled with smoke. Then said I, Woe is me! for I am undone; because I am a man of unclean lips, and I dwell in the midst of a people of unclean lips: for mine eyes have seen the King, the LORD of hosts."
(Think about each word while rereading)

**Meditatio:** Reread everything
(Pause for at least 30 seconds to absorb everything)

**Oratio:** "Forgive me! for I am undone; God I am a man of unclean lips, and I dwell in the middle of a people of unclean lips: reveal to me more of YOU God, let me see your glory LORD of hosts."
(Repeat three times)

**Contemplatio:** Reread everything once
(Pause at least 30 seconds to consider deeper meanings)


What are you thinking?

Write what you're thinking, anything, no matter what it is, write your thought in the space below:

Whether you think you heard from God or not, go over the quote and Scriptio a final time and finish it off with an amen.
Then go about your day.

# TABLE OF CONTENTS

# CHRIST IN THE STILLNESS
## WEEK ONE

Colin Rex - Grafarkirkja, Iceland

There are times when we just don't know what God wants from us. For you these moments might be rare, or as with me, they might happen often. Though just because we are lost, or the Spirit is restless inside of us, doesn't mean that God isn't working. It doesn't mean the Spirit isn't moving. It just means we can't figure it out, or maybe we just can't hear it. Whatever the case may be, I have noticed that when the storm inside of me is raging, often times, outside in the real world, things are still, maybe even too calm. That might even be what is causing your angst, that it feels like there is nothing for you to do, or no place for you to fit into.

**These are times we need to Seek Christ Through the Stillness!**

## WEEK ONE | DAY ONE

**Lectio:** "It was a daring prayer offered by Augustine when he said "Lord hast Thou declared that no man shall see Thy face and live? -Then let me die, That I may see Thee." -Stanford
(Think about each word while rereading)

**Scriptio:** Isaiah 6:1-3 "In the year that king Uzziah died I saw also the LORD sitting upon a throne, high and lifted up, and his train filled the temple. Above it stood the seraphim: each one had six wings; with two he covered his face, and with two he covered his feet, and with two he did fly. And one cried unto another, and said, Holy, holy, holy, is the LORD of hosts: the whole earth is full of his glory."
(Think about each word while rereading)

**Meditatio:** Reread everything
(Pause for at least 30 seconds to absorb everything)

**Oratio:** "Holy, Holy, Holy, ARE YOU LORD of hosts: the whole earth is full of YOUR glory!"
(Repeat three times)

**Contemplatio:** Reread everything once
(Pause at least 30 seconds to consider deeper meanings)


What are you thinking?

Write what you're thinking, anything, no matter what it is, write your thought in the space below:


Now go on with your day!

## WEEK ONE | DAY TWO

**Lectio:** "It was a daring prayer offered by Augustine when he said "Lord hast Thou declared that no man shall see Thy face and live? -Then let me die, That I may see Thee."
-Stanford
(Think about each word while rereading)

**Scriptio:** Isaiah 6:4-5 "And the posts of the door moved at the voice of him that cried, and the house was filled with smoke. Then said I, Woe is me! for I am undone; because I am a man of unclean lips, and I dwell in the midst of a people of unclean lips: for mine eyes have seen the King, the LORD of hosts."
(Think about each word while rereading)

**Meditatio:** Reread everything
(Pause for at least 30 seconds to absorb everything)

**Oratio:** "Forgive me! for I am undone; God I am a man of unclean lips, and I dwell in the middle of a people of unclean lips: reveal to me more of YOU God, let me see your glory LORD of hosts."
(Repeat three times)

**Contemplatio:** Reread everything once
(Pause at least 30 seconds to consider deeper meanings)


What are you thinking?

Write what you're thinking, anything, no matter what it is, write your thought in the space below:




Now go on with your day!

## WEEK ONE | DAY THREE

**Lectio:** "It was a daring prayer offered by Augustine when he said "Lord hast Thou declared that no man shall see Thy face and live? -Then let me die, That I may see Thee." -Stanford
(Think about each word while rereading)

**Scriptio:** Isaiah 6:6-7 "Then flew one of the seraphim unto me, having a live coal in his hand, which he had taken with the tongs from off the altar: And he laid it upon my mouth, and said, Lo, this has touched your lips; and your iniquity [great sins] is taken away, and your sin purged."
(Think about each word while rereading)

**Meditatio:** Reread everything
(Pause for at least 30 seconds to absorb everything)

**Oratio:** "Lord God touch my lips; take my iniquity away, purge me of my sin that I may only speak your praises."
(Repeat three times)

**Contemplatio:** Reread everything once
(Pause at least 30 seconds to consider deeper meanings)

What are you thinking?

Write what you're thinking, anything, no matter what it is, write your thought in the space below:

Now go on with your day!

## WEEK ONE | DAY FOUR

**Lectio:** "It was a daring prayer offered by Augustine when he said "Lord hast Thou declared that no man shall see Thy face and live? -Then let me die, That I may see Thee."
-Stanford
(Think about each word while rereading)

**Scriptio:** Isaiah 6:8 "Also I heard the voice of the Lord, saying, Whom shall I send, and who will go for us? Then said I, Here am I; send me. "
(Think about each word while rereading)

**Meditatio:** Reread everything
(Pause for at least 30 seconds to absorb everything)

**Oratio:** "Lord God speak to me that I may tremble in your presence; Whom shall You send, and who will go for You? I declare, Here am I; Lord send me. I declare, Here am I; Lord use me for YOUR glory."
(Repeat three times)

**Contemplatio:** Reread everything once
(Pause at least 30 seconds to consider deeper meanings)


What are you thinking?

Write what you're thinking, anything, no matter what it is, write your thought in the space below:




Now go on with your day!

## WEEK ONE | DAY FIVE

**Lectio:** "It was a daring prayer offered by Augustine when he said "Lord hast Thou declared that no man shall see Thy face and live? -Then let me die, That I may see Thee." -Stanford
(Think about each word while rereading)

**Scriptio:** Isaiah 6:9-10 "And he said, Go, and tell this people, Hear all of you indeed, but understand not; and see all of you indeed, but perceive not. Make the heart of this people fat, and make their ears heavy, and shut their eyes; lest they see with their eyes, and hear with their ears, and understand with their heart, and convert, and be healed."
(Think about each word while rereading)

**Meditatio:** Reread everything
(Pause for at least 30 seconds to absorb everything)

**Oratio:** "Lord God help me to go where you tell me to go. Help me to hear your voice. Help me to understand. Help me to see. Help me to know you.  Heal my heart. Heal my soul. Heal me Lord."
(Repeat three times)

**Contemplatio:** Reread everything once
(Pause at least 30 seconds to consider deeper meanings)


What are you thinking?

Write what you're thinking, anything, no matter what it is, write your thought in the space below:



Now go on with your day!

## WEEK ONE | DAY SIX

**Lectio:** "It was a daring prayer offered by Augustine when he said "Lord hast Thou declared that no man shall see Thy face and live? -Then let me die, That I may see Thee."
-Stanford
(Think about each word while rereading)

**Scriptio:** Isaiah 6:11-12 "Then said I, Lord, how long? And he answered, Until the cities be wasted without inhabitant, and the houses without man, and the land be utterly desolate, And the LORD have removed men far away, and there be a great forsaking in the midst of the land."
(Think about each word while rereading)

**Meditatio:** Reread everything
(Pause for at least 30 seconds to absorb everything)

**Oratio:** "Dear God help me not to forget you. Forgive me for wasting any part of my life. Restore my desolate heart. You HAVE removed my shame. Help me to never forsake you. Thank you for loving me."
(Repeat three times)

**Contemplatio:** Reread everything once
(Pause at least 30 seconds to consider deeper meanings)


What are you thinking?

Write what you're thinking, anything, no matter what it is, write your thought in the space below:




Now go on with your day!

## WEEK ONE | DAY SEVEN

**Lectio:** "It was a daring prayer offered by Augustine when he said "Lord hast Thou declared that no man shall see Thy face and live? -Then let me die, That I may see Thee." -Stanford
(Think about each word while rereading)

**Scriptio:** Isaiah 6:13 "But yet in it shall be a tenth, and it shall return, and shall be eaten: as a teil tree, and as an oak, whose substance is in them, when they cast their leaves: so the holy seed shall be the substance thereof.
(Think about each word while rereading)

**Meditatio:** Reread everything
(Pause for at least 30 seconds to absorb everything)

**Oratio:** "Lord God You always preserve a remnant. Thank You for Your mercy. Grow my faith like an oak. Let my substance be filled with You. Thank you for filling me with Your Spirit. May the seedling of my faith continue to grow in you."
(Repeat three times)

**Contemplatio:** Reread everything once
(Pause at least 30 seconds to consider deeper meanings)

What are you thinking?

Write what you're thinking, anything, no matter what it is, write your thought in the space below:


It is the seventh day, a day of rest, so try to relax in knowing Jesus loves you more than His own life!

He died so that you may live, and make the most of every moment!

# CHRIST IN THE LONELINESS
## WEEK TWO

Liam Simpson-Aoraki/Mount Cook National Park, New Zealand

In the middle of chaos we are often the most alone. Whether because the chaos pushed others away or we pushed others away. Either way, it is in those moments we can feel so small in this huge world.

**These are times we need to Seek Christ Through the Stillness!**

## WEEK TWO | DAY ONE

**Lectio:** "Four-year-old Martha, hugging a doll in each of her pudgy little arms, looked wistfully up at her mother and said, "Mama, I love them and love them and love them, but they never love me back."
-Jeanette W. Lockerbie
(Think about each word while rereading)

**Scriptio:** Matthew 10:16 "Behold, I send you forth as sheep in the midst of wolves: be all of you therefore wise as serpents, and harmless as doves."
(Think about each word while rereading)

**Meditatio:** Reread everything
(Pause for at least 30 seconds to absorb everything)

**Oratio:** "Jesus send me forth and give me courage. Teach me peace. Guide me in wisdom. Help me not to bruise any of your children."
(Repeat three times)

**Contemplatio:** Reread everything once
(Pause at least 30 seconds to consider deeper meanings)


What are you thinking?

Write what you're thinking, anything, no matter what it is, write your thought in the space below:




Now go on with your day!

## WEEK TWO | DAY TWO

**Lectio:** "Four-year-old Martha, hugging a doll in each of her pudgy little arms, looked wistfully up at her mother and said, "Mama, I love them and love them and love them, but they never love me back."
-Jeanette W. Lockerbie
(Think about each word while rereading)

**Scriptio:** Matthew 10:17 "But beware of men: for they will deliver you up to the councils, and they will scourge you in their synagogues;"
(Think about each word while rereading)

**Meditatio:** Reread everything
(Pause for at least 30 seconds to absorb everything)

**Oratio:** "Jesus give me the courage to stand strong for You. I will go where you send me. Protect me on my path and calm my restless heart."
(Repeat three times)

**Contemplatio:** Reread everything once
(Pause at least 30 seconds to consider deeper meanings)


What are you thinking?

Write what you're thinking, anything, no matter what it is, write your thought in the space below:




Now go on with your day!

## WEEK TWO | DAY THREE

**Lectio:** "Four-year-old Martha, hugging a doll in each of her pudgy little arms, looked wistfully up at her mother and said, "Mama, I love them and love them and love them, but they never love me back."
-Jeanette W. Lockerbie
(Think about each word while rereading)

**Scriptio:** Matthew 10:18 "And all of you shall be brought before governors and kings for my sake, for a testimony against them and the Gentiles."
(Think about each word while rereading)

**Meditatio:** Reread everything
(Pause for at least 30 seconds to absorb everything)

**Oratio:** "Jesus let me be a testimony for You. Teach me what you desire me to know. Let The Holy Spirit speak through me. May I be ready to be the vessel used for Your Glory."
(Repeat three times)

**Contemplatio:** Reread everything once
(Pause at least 30 seconds to consider deeper meanings)


What are you thinking?

Write what you're thinking, anything, no matter what it is, write your thought in the space below:




Now go on with your day!

## WEEK TWO | DAY FOUR

**Lectio:** "Four-year-old Martha, hugging a doll in each of her pudgy little arms, looked wistfully up at her mother and said, "Mama, I love them and love them and love them, but they never love me back."
-Jeanette W. Lockerbie
(Think about each word while rereading)

**Scriptio:** Matthew 10:19 "But when they deliver you up, take no thought how or what all of you shall speak: for it shall be given you in that same hour what all of you shall speak."
(Think about each word while rereading)

**Meditatio:** Reread everything
(Pause for at least 30 seconds to absorb everything)

**Oratio:** "Jesus speak through me. Give me the words. I am limited without You. Teach me Your ways. Show me how to extend grace and mercy."
(Repeat three times)

**Contemplatio:** Reread everything once
(Pause at least 30 seconds to consider deeper meanings)


What are you thinking?

Write what you're thinking, anything, no matter what it is, write your thought in the space below:




Now go on with your day!

## WEEK TWO | DAY FIVE

**Lectio:** "Four-year-old Martha, hugging a doll in each of her pudgy little arms, looked wistfully up at her mother and said, "Mama, I love them and love them and love them, but they never love me back."
-Jeanette W. Lockerbie
(Think about each word while rereading)

**Scriptio:** Matthew 10:20 "For it is not ye that speak, but the Spirit of your Father which speaks in you."
(Think about each word while rereading)

**Meditatio:** Reread everything
(Pause for at least 30 seconds to absorb everything)

**Oratio:** "Lord Jesus give me the words to praise you. Give the ability to reach someone for You. I will go where you send me. Speak through me."
(Repeat three times)

**Contemplatio:** Reread everything once
(Pause at least 30 seconds to consider deeper meanings)

What are you thinking?

Write what you're thinking, anything, no matter what it is, write your thought in the space below:

Now go on with your day!

## WEEK TWO | DAY SIX

**Lectio:** "Four-year-old Martha, hugging a doll in each of her pudgy little arms, looked wistfully up at her mother and said, "Mama, I love them and love them and love them, but they never love me back."
-Jeanette W. Lockerbie
(Think about each word while rereading)

**Scriptio:** Matthew 10:21 "And the brother shall deliver up the brother to death, and the father the child: and the children shall rise up against their parents, and cause them to be put to death."
(Think about each word while rereading)

**Meditatio:** Reread everything
(Pause for at least 30 seconds to absorb everything)

**Oratio:** "Jesus teach me to control my emotions. Work on me from the inside out. So that even if I am hated, I will show Your endless love. Fill my soul with your calming presence."
(Repeat three times)

**Contemplatio:** Reread everything once
(Pause at least 30 seconds to consider deeper meanings)


What are you thinking?

Write what you're thinking, anything, no matter what it is, write your thought in the space below:




Now go on with your day!

## WEEK TWO | DAY SEVEN

**Lectio:** "Four-year-old Martha, hugging a doll in each of her pudgy little arms, looked wistfully up at her mother and said, "Mama, I love them and love them and love them, but they never love me back."
-Jeanette W. Lockerbie
(Think about each word while rereading)

**Scriptio:** Matthew 10:22 "And ye shall be hated of all men for my name's sake: but he that endures to the end shall be saved."
(Think about each word while rereading)

**Meditatio:** Reread everything
(Pause for at least 30 seconds to absorb everything)

**Oratio:** "Jesus I am too weak to do this alone. Give me the strength. The strength to go through this; to do the good you would have me do. Help me to not care what the world has to say. Show me how to reach Your lost sheep. Only You Jesus! Make me so that You are all I see! Help me endure."
(Repeat three times)

**Contemplatio:** Reread everything once
(Pause at least 30 seconds to consider deeper meanings)

What are you thinking?

Write what you're thinking, anything, no matter what it is, write your thought in the space below:




It is the seventh day, a day of rest, so try to relax in knowing Jesus saved you before you knew Him!

He died so that you may live, and make the most of every moment!

# CHRIST IN THE WITNESS
## WEEK THREE

Samuel Scrimshaw

There are times, most of my life, when you are lonely in a crowd, you feel isolated within yourself, and you feel cold and numb to the spiritual side of life. But if you look around there are others who feel this way also, in fact, there are others who are in far worse situations that seem completely okay with their situation. Feelings, they are strange thing, feelings, they are real to the person feeling them, even if completely wrong to the world outside of your head. And if you are wanting to move outside of your feelings, and help yourself, go help someone else.

**You might be surprised how helping someone else might be the help YOU really needed after all.**

## WEEK THREE | DAY ONE

**Lectio:** St. Ambrose says that a Christian wife was on a journey with her heathen husband, when a terrific thunder storm rose, which overwhelmed the man with terror. His wife asked the cause. He replied, "Are you not afraid?" she answered, "No, not at all: For I know that it is the voice of my heavenly father; and shall a child be afraid of her father's voice?" The husband saw that his wife had what he had not; and this led him to the adoption of Christianity. -- Foster
(Think about each word while rereading)

**Scriptio:** 1 Corinthians 7:12-13 "But to the rest speak I, not the Lord: If any brother has a wife that believes not, and she be pleased to dwell with him, let him not put her away. And the woman which has a husband that believes not, and if he be pleased to dwell with her, let her not leave him."
(Think about each word while rereading)

**Meditatio:** Reread everything
(Pause for at least 30 seconds to absorb everything)

**Oratio:** "Jesus help me to love others with even a fraction of how You love reprobate like me. Continue to build me. Make me new again."
(Repeat three times)

**Contemplatio:** Reread everything once
(Pause at least 30 seconds to consider deeper meanings)

What are you thinking?

Write what you're thinking, anything, no matter what it is, write your thought in the space below:

Now go on with your day!

## WEEK THREE | DAY TWO

**Lectio:** St. Ambrose says that a Christian wife was on a journey with her heathen husband, when a terrific thunder storm rose, which overwhelmed the man with terror. His wife asked the cause. He replied, "Are you not afraid?" she answered, "No, not at all: For I know that it is the voice of my heavenly father; and shall a child be afraid of her father's voice?" The husband saw that his wife had what he had not; and this led him to the adoption of Christianity. -- Foster
(Think about each word while rereading)

**Scriptio:** 1 Corinthians 7:14 "For the unbelieving husband is sanctified by the wife, and the unbelieving wife is sanctified by the husband: else were your children unclean; but now are they holy."
(Think about each word while rereading)

**Meditatio:** Reread everything
(Pause for at least 30 seconds to absorb everything)

**Oratio:** "Help me! Guide me so that I can guide the one you gave me. I want to be the best spouse I can be. But I'm selfish, do with me what You will!"
(Repeat three times)

**Contemplatio:** Reread everything once
(Pause at least 30 seconds to consider deeper meanings)

What are you thinking?

Write what you're thinking, anything, no matter what it is, write your thought in the space below:

Now go on with your day!

## WEEK THREE | DAY THREE

**Lectio:** St. Ambrose says that a Christian wife was on a journey with her heathen husband, when a terrific thunder storm rose, which overwhelmed the man with terror. His wife asked the cause. He replied, "Are you not afraid?" she answered, "No, not at all: For I know that it is the voice of my heavenly father; and shall a child be afraid of her father's voice?" The husband saw that his wife had what he had not; and this led him to the adoption of Christianity.
-- Foster
(Think about each word while rereading)

**Scriptio:** 1 Corinthians 7:15 "But if the unbelieving depart, let him depart. A brother or a sister is not under bondage in such cases: but God has called us to peace."
(Think about each word while rereading)

**Meditatio:** Reread everything
(Pause for at least 30 seconds to absorb everything)

**Oratio**: "Help me to be okay with failure. Help me to let go. Be my shield over my heart, that I can love without fear. A True love, Your Love."
(Repeat three times)

**Contemplatio:** Reread everything once
(Pause at least 30 seconds to consider deeper meanings)

What are you thinking?

Write what you're thinking, anything, no matter what it is, write your thought in the space below:

Now go on with your day!

## WEEK THREE | DAY FOUR

**Lectio:** St. Ambrose says that a Christian wife was on a journey with her heathen husband, when a terrific thunder storm rose, which overwhelmed the man with terror. His wife asked the cause. He replied, "Are you not afraid?" she answered, "No, not at all: For I know that it is the voice of my heavenly father; and shall a child be afraid of her father's voice?" The husband saw that his wife had what he had not; and this led him to the adoption of Christianity. -- Foster
(Think about each word while rereading)

**Scriptio:** 1 Corinthians 7:16 "For what know you, O wife, whether you shall save your husband? Or how know you, O man, whether you shall save your wife?"
(Think about each word while rereading)

**Meditatio:** Reread everything
(Pause for at least 30 seconds to absorb everything)

**Oratio**: "Jesus you use the simple things to confound the wise. May I never be too wise to ask You for help. And may my loving wife always have a faithful husband. And help me love her the way you made her!"
(Repeat three times)

**Contemplatio:** Reread everything once
(Pause at least 30 seconds to consider deeper meanings)

What are you thinking?

Write what you're thinking, anything, no matter what it is, write your thought in the space below:

Now go on with your day!

## WEEK THREE | DAY FIVE

**Lectio:** St. Ambrose says that a Christian wife was on a journey with her heathen husband, when a terrific thunder storm rose, which overwhelmed the man with terror. His wife asked the cause. He replied, "Are you not afraid?" she answered, "No, not at all: For I know that it is the voice of my heavenly father; and shall a child be afraid of her father's voice?" The husband saw that his wife had what he had not; and this led him to the adoption of Christianity. -- Foster
(Think about each word while rereading)

**Scriptio:** 1 Corinthians 7:17 "But as God has distributed to every man, as the Lord has called every one, so let him walk. And so ordain I in all churches."
(Think about each word while rereading)

**Meditatio:** Reread everything
(Pause for at least 30 seconds to absorb everything)

**Oratio**: "May I learn to always find joy in doing your service. Help me to stay in your grace, even when I feel like I can't continue. Be my strength."
(Repeat three times)

**Contemplatio:** Reread everything once
(Pause at least 30 seconds to consider deeper meanings)

What are you thinking?

Write what you're thinking, anything, no matter what it is, write your thought in the space below:

Now go on with your day!

## WEEK THREE | DAY SIX

**Lectio:** St. Ambrose says that a Christian wife was on a journey with her heathen husband, when a terrific thunder storm rose, which overwhelmed the man with terror. His wife asked the cause. He replied, "Are you not afraid?" she answered, "No, not at all: For I know that it is the voice of my heavenly father; and shall a child be afraid of her father's voice?" The husband saw that his wife had what he had not; and this led him to the adoption of Christianity. -- Foster
(Think about each word while rereading)

**Scriptio:** 1 Corinthians 7:18-19 "Is any man called being circumcised? let him not become uncircumcised. Is any called in uncircumcision? let him not be circumcised. Circumcision is nothing, and uncircumcision is nothing, but the keeping of the commandments of God."
(Think about each word while rereading)

**Meditatio:** Reread everything
(Pause for at least 30 seconds to absorb everything)

**Oratio**: "May I always value your Word over my want. Help me love."
(Repeat three times)

**Contemplatio:** Reread everything once
(Pause at least 30 seconds to consider deeper meanings)

What are you thinking?

Write what you're thinking, anything, no matter what it is, write your thought in the space below:

Now go on with your day!

## WEEK THREE | DAY SEVEN

**Lectio:** St. Ambrose says that a Christian wife was on a journey with her heathen husband, when a terrific thunder storm rose, which overwhelmed the man with terror. His wife asked the cause. He replied, "Are you not afraid?" she answered, "No, not at all: For I know that it is the voice of my heavenly father; and shall a child be afraid of her father's voice?" The husband saw that his wife had what he had not; and this led him to the adoption of Christianity. -- Foster
(Think about each word while rereading)

**Scriptio:** 1 Corinthians 7:20-23 "Let every man abide in the same calling wherein he was called. Are you called being a servant? care not for it: but if you may be made free, use it rather. For he that is called in the Lord, being a servant, is the Lord's freeman: likewise, also he that is called, being free, is Christ's servant. All of you are bought with a price"
(Think about each word while rereading)

**Meditatio:** Reread everything
(Pause for at least 30 seconds to absorb everything)

**Oratio**: "Jesus, oh, what a price you paid! Jesus be my center. Help me continue to develop a servant's heart. Create in me what You want of me."
(Repeat three times)

**Contemplatio:** Reread everything once
(Pause at least 30 seconds to consider deeper meanings)

What are you thinking?

Write what you're thinking, anything, no matter what it is, write your thought in the space below:

It is the seventh day, a day of rest, so try to relax in knowing Jesus loves you even if you don't love yourself!

# CHRIST IN THE DARKNESS
## WEEK FOUR

Peter Winckler - Québec City, Canada

Sometimes no matter how much you push against the darkness, no matter how much you pray about it, try to feel better, you just don't. You just do not feel any better. And nothing can console you, nothing makes it better. You want to be away from everything, and you no longer enjoy anything you used to. How could you? You don't even like yourself. Welcome to my life. But you have to just get up anyway. You have to make yourself put on your clothes, get your socks and shoes on, and go face the world. You force yourself to go to work, to go to the store, to do the things in life that are expected. And even though it does not get better, it can get easier. Just push yourself.

**Embrace Christ IN the Darkness, because He is there. It's up to you to grab a hold of Him.**

## WEEK FOUR | DAY ONE

**Lectio:** "I'd rather light a candle than curse the darkness"
-- James Kelly
(Think about each word while rereading)

**Scriptio:** Psalm 27:1 "The Lord is my light and my salvation; whom shall I fear? the Lord is the strength of my life; of whom shall I be afraid?"
(Think about each word while rereading)

**Meditatio:** Reread everything
(Pause for at least 30 seconds to absorb everything)

**Oratio:** "Lord God, you are the Great I AM. The Living God! Be my light. Hold me through the darkness. I fear my own works. My soul is dirty. Cleanse me Jesus. Holy Spirit give me strength that I do not have on my own. Calm my heart when I have moments of fear and doubt creeps in."
(Repeat three times)

**Contemplatio:** Reread everything once
(Pause at least 30 seconds to consider deeper meanings)


What are you thinking?

Write what you're thinking, anything, no matter what it is, write your thought in the space below:



Now go on with your day!

## WEEK FOUR | DAY TWO

**Lectio:** "I'd rather light a candle than curse the darkness"
-- James Kelly
(Think about each word while rereading)

**Scriptio:** Psalm 27:2-3 "When the wicked, even mine enemies and my foes, came upon me to eat up my flesh, they stumbled and fell. Though a host should encamp against me, my heart shall not fear: though war should rise against me, in this will I be confident."
(Think about each word while rereading)

**Meditatio:** Reread everything
(Pause for at least 30 seconds to absorb everything)

**Oratio:** "God, work in my soul that I can become more like You. I feel so far from you when I think of Your Goodness. I have made enemies by being foolish, help me to end my foolishness and make peace with those I've hurt. Forgive me for being so far, when you have made it so easy."
(Repeat three times)

**Contemplatio:** Reread everything once
(Pause at least 30 seconds to consider deeper meanings)


What are you thinking?

Write what you're thinking, anything, no matter what it is, write your thought in the space below:




Now go on with your day!

## WEEK FOUR | DAY THREE

**Lectio:** "I'd rather light a candle than curse the darkness"
-- James Kelly
(Think about each word while rereading)

**Scriptio:** Psalm 27:4 "One thing have I desired of the Lord, that will I seek after; that I may dwell in the house of the Lord all the days of my life, to behold the beauty of the Lord, and to enquire in his temple."
(Think about each word while rereading)

**Meditatio:** Reread everything
(Pause for at least 30 seconds to absorb everything)

**Oratio:** "My God, I long to feel the warmth of your love, to sit beside you and feel your awesome slender. Your righteousness brings me to tears. The space between where I am and where you are is so great. Thank you for making me your temple, though I am unworthy of such an indwelling. Work on my heart, make me more like you, I pray you change me for good. Continue the work you started until I am worthy of your presence."
(Repeat three times)

**Contemplatio:** Reread everything once
(Pause at least 30 seconds to consider deeper meanings)


What are you thinking?

Write what you're thinking, anything, no matter what it is, write your thought in the space below:


Now go on with your day!

## WEEK FOUR | DAY FOUR

**Lectio:** "I'd rather light a candle than curse the darkness"
-- James Kelly
(Think about each word while rereading)

**Scriptio:** Psalm 27:5 "For in the time of trouble he shall
hide me in his pavilion: in the secret of his tabernacle shall
he hide me; he shall set me up upon a rock."
(Think about each word while rereading)

**Meditatio:** Reread everything
(Pause for at least 30 seconds to absorb everything)

**Oratio:** "Lord thank you for your protection. I need you
more and more every day. May I never start to think I don't
need you. Jesus thank you for being my Rock. My fortress
against the evil that I have caused. Keep working on me
as long as I live that I might prepare the ground for untold
numbers of people to yield to you."
(Repeat three times)

**Contemplatio:** Reread everything once
(Pause at least 30 seconds to consider deeper meanings)


What are you thinking?

Write what you're thinking, anything, no matter what it is,
write your thought in the space below:




Now go on with your day!

## WEEK FOUR | DAY FIVE

**Lectio:** "I'd rather light a candle than curse the darkness"
-- James Kelly
(Think about each word while rereading)

**Scriptio:** Psalm 27:6 "And now shall mine head be lifted up above mine enemies round about me: therefore, will I offer in his tabernacle sacrifices of joy; I will sing, yea, I will sing praises unto the Lord."
(Think about each word while rereading)

**Meditatio:** Reread everything
(Pause for at least 30 seconds to absorb everything)

**Oratio:** "My Lord, though I struggle against your will. I still love You. Remember me when you are separating the sheep and goats. Though I don't always show it, You know I love you. I will gladly die for you Lord, but help me to live for you! I want to be Yours!"
(Repeat three times)

**Contemplatio:** Reread everything once
(Pause at least 30 seconds to consider deeper meanings)


What are you thinking?

Write what you're thinking, anything, no matter what it is, write your thought in the space below:




Now go on with your day!

## WEEK FOUR | DAY SIX

**Lectio:** "I'd rather light a candle than curse the darkness"
-- James Kelly
(Think about each word while rereading)

**Scriptio:** Psalm 27:7-8 "Hear, O Lord, when I cry with my voice: have mercy also upon me, and answer me. When thou said, Seek ye my face; my heart said unto thee, Thy face, Lord, will I seek."
(Think about each word while rereading)

**Meditatio:** Reread everything
(Pause for at least 30 seconds to absorb everything)

**Oratio:** "God though the darkness is all around me, Lord help me not to grow bitter. Through many disappointments of my own making, help me not to forget You bought me. Jesus, when no one else wanted me, you paid everything for me. Thank you."
(Repeat three times)

**Contemplatio:** Reread everything once
(Pause at least 30 seconds to consider deeper meanings)


What are you thinking?

Write what you're thinking, anything, no matter what it is, write your thought in the space below:




Now go on with your day!

## WEEK FOUR | DAY SEVEN

**Lectio:** "I'd rather light a candle than curse the darkness"
-- James Kelly
(Think about each word while rereading)

**Scriptio:** Psalm 27:9 "Hide not Your face far from me; put not Your servant away in anger: You have been my help; leave me not, neither forsake me, O God of my salvation."
(Think about each word while rereading)

**Meditatio:** Reread everything
(Pause for at least 30 seconds to absorb everything)

**Oratio:** "Jesus, Jesus, Jesus. I AM, YHWH, El Shaddai, LORD, Adonai, HaShem, Immanuel, Messiah, Christ, Yehoshua, God is Salvation, Yeshua, God's Salvation. You are truly so great no name can describe You! You are the Bread of Life, The Rock of my salvation, my Redeemer, and my shelter from the coming storm. Keep me, even when I drift, keep me. Breath on me."
(Repeat three times)

**Contemplatio:** Reread everything once
(Pause at least 30 seconds to consider deeper meanings)

What are you thinking?

Write what you're thinking, anything, no matter what it is, write your thought in the space below:

It is the seventh day, a day of rest, so try to relax in knowing Jesus loves you and paid your penalty, before you knew Him!

# CHRIST IN THE CHAOS
## WEEK FIVE

Jared Rice - Yucatan, Mexico

There are times when we just don't want to continue living. The storms and chaos can be, at times, too much to bear. As someone who struggles with depression, I have often felt it is better to die than live. Sadly, the most chaotic moments of our lives are usually the product of our own creation. We bring it upon ourselves in the way that we act, react, treat others, and most often, how we ignore the Holy Spirit and His pulling. We react carnally to mental, emotional, and often spiritual stimuli.
Still that does not make it easier to handle, and when your heart feels like it's going to burst, that is the moment to cling tightest to Christ, the great I AM, our ever-present savior in times of distress.

**These are times we need to Seek Christ Through the Chaos!**

## WEEK FIVE | DAY ONE

**Lectio:** "A New York newspaper had this story: 'the body of a man about 70 years old was recovered from the Spuyten Duyvil Creek yesterday. Police found this note: 'I'm Joe Barnes. No record. No permanent address. No relatives. No friends. Just tired of living.' That is the sad obituary of a man overcome..."
-- Ray O. Jones
(Think about each word while rereading)

**Scriptio:** Psalm 77:1-2 "I cried unto God with my voice, even unto God with my voice; and he gave ear unto me. In the day of my trouble I sought the Lord: my sore ran in the night, and ceased not: my soul refused to be comforted."
(Think about each word while rereading)

**Meditatio:** Reread everything
(Pause for at least 30 seconds to absorb everything)

**Oratio:** "Lord wipe my tears and hear my voice. Let me be open with You. I'm in pain over the future. I can't be comforted, but please be with me."
(Repeat three times)

**Contemplatio:** Reread everything once
(Pause at least 30 seconds to consider deeper meanings)

What are you thinking?

Write what you're thinking, anything, no matter what it is, write your thought in the space below:

Now go on with your day!

## WEEK FIVE | DAY TWO

**Lectio:** "A New York newspaper had this story: 'the body of a man about 70 years old was recovered from the Spuyten Duyvil Creek yesterday. Police found this note: 'I'm Joe Barnes. No record. No permanent address. No relatives. No friends. Just tired of living.' That is the sad obituary of a man overcome..."
-- Ray O. Jones
(Think about each word while rereading)

**Scriptio:** Psalm 77:3 "I remembered God, and was troubled: I complained, and my spirit was overwhelmed. Selah."
(Think about each word while rereading)

**Meditatio:** Reread everything
(Pause for at least 30 seconds to absorb everything)

**Oratio:** "I remember You God, I fear your wrath over my shortcomings. Hear my whines, but know my heart. I want more of you! But I'm weak. Please fill me I am overwhelmed."
(Repeat three times)

**Contemplatio:** Reread everything once
(Pause at least 30 seconds to consider deeper meanings)


What are you thinking?

Write what you're thinking, anything, no matter what it is, write your thought in the space below:




Now go on with your day!

## WEEK FIVE | DAY THREE

**Lectio:** "A New York newspaper had this story: 'the body of a man about 70 years old was recovered from the Spuyten Duyvil Creek yesterday. Police found this note: 'I'm Joe Barnes. No record. No permanent address. No relatives. No friends. Just tired of living.' That is the sad obituary of a man overcome..."
-- Ray O. Jones
(Think about each word while rereading)

**Scriptio:** Psalm 77:4 "You hold mine eyes waking: I am so troubled that I cannot speak."
(Think about each word while rereading)

**Meditatio:** Reread everything
(Pause for at least 30 seconds to absorb everything)

**Oratio:** "YHWH, YHWH, YHWH, The Great I AM. Lord of Hosts. You are silent, not giving me peace. Please speak to me. I am so troubled I can't find words. Give me words. Give me peace."
(Repeat three times)

**Contemplatio:** Reread everything once
(Pause at least 30 seconds to consider deeper meanings)


What are you thinking?

Write what you're thinking, anything, no matter what it is, write your thought in the space below:



Now go on with your day!

## WEEK FIVE | DAY FOUR

**Lectio:** "A New York newspaper had this story: 'the body of a man about 70 years old was recovered from the Spuyten Duyvil Creek yesterday. Police found this note: 'I'm Joe Barnes. No record. No permanent address. No relatives. No friends. Just tired of living.' That is the sad obituary of a man overcome..."
-- Ray O. Jones
(Think about each word while rereading)

**Scriptio:** Psalm 77:5-6 "I have considered the days of old, the years of ancient times. I call to remembrance my song in the night: I commune with mine own heart: and my spirit made diligent search."
(Think about each word while rereading)

**Meditatio:** Reread everything
(Pause for at least 30 seconds to absorb everything)

**Oratio:** "Lord I remember my past, when I was sure of your plan. I will sing songs of your greatness. I will tell myself to remember Your greatness. I will search my heart and mind to remember Your Goodness."
(Repeat three times)

**Contemplatio:** Reread everything once
(Pause at least 30 seconds to consider deeper meanings)


What are you thinking?

Write what you're thinking, anything, no matter what it is, write your thought in the space below:


Now go on with your day!

## WEEK FIVE | DAY FIVE

**Lectio:** "A New York newspaper had this story: 'the body of a man about 70 years old was recovered from the Spuyten Duyvil Creek yesterday. Police found this note: 'I'm Joe Barnes. No record. No permanent address. No relatives. No friends. Just tired of living.' That is the sad obituary of a man overcome..."
-- Ray O. Jones
(Think about each word while rereading)

**Scriptio:** Psalm 77:7-8 "Will the Lord cast off for ever? and will he be favorable no more? Is his mercy clean gone for ever? does his promise fail for evermore?"
(Think about each word while rereading)

**Meditatio:** Reread everything
(Pause for at least 30 seconds to absorb everything)

**Oratio:** "Will You stay silent forever? How long before you remember me and give me peace? I feel like you will never help again. I know you never fail, so give me strength to follow, even when I don't understand."
(Repeat three times)

**Contemplatio:** Reread everything once
(Pause at least 30 seconds to consider deeper meanings)


What are you thinking?

Write what you're thinking, anything, no matter what it is, write your thought in the space below:




Now go on with your day!

## WEEK FIVE | DAY SIX

**Lectio:** "A New York newspaper had this story: 'the body of a man about 70 years old was recovered from the Spuyten Duyvil Creek yesterday. Police found this note: 'I'm Joe Barnes. No record. No permanent address. No relatives. No friends. Just tired of living.' That is the sad obituary of a man overcome..."
-- Ray O. Jones
(Think about each word while rereading)

**Scriptio:** Psalm 77:9-10 "Has God forgotten to be gracious? has he in anger shut up his tender mercies? Selah. And I said, This is my infirmity: but I will remember the years of the right hand of the most High."
(Think about each word while rereading)

**Meditatio:** Reread everything
(Pause for at least 30 seconds to absorb everything)

**Oratio:** "Lord I know you will never fail to be graceful. But I feel the heat of your anger toward me. Be gentle with me. I am nothing on my own. I remember the times you have favored me. You are so good!"
(Repeat three times)

**Contemplatio:** Reread everything once
(Pause at least 30 seconds to consider deeper meanings)


What are you thinking?

Write what you're thinking, anything, no matter what it is, write your thought in the space below:



Now go on with your day!

## WEEK FIVE | DAY SEVEN

**Lectio:** "A New York newspaper had this story: 'the body of a man about 70 years old was recovered from the Spuyten Duyvil Creek yesterday. Police found this note: 'I'm Joe Barnes. No record. No permanent address. No relatives. No friends. Just tired of living.' That is the sad obituary of a man overcome..."
-- Ray O. Jones
(Think about each word while rereading)

**Scriptio:** Psalm 77:11-14 "I will remember the works of the LORD: surely I will remember your wonders of old. I will meditate also of all your work, and talk of your doings. Your way, O God, is in the sanctuary: who is so great a God as our God? You are the God that do wonders: you have declared your strength among the people." (Think about each word while rereading)

**Meditatio:** Reread everything
(Pause for at least 30 seconds to absorb everything)

**Oratio:** "God, in my turmoil I remember you are great. You are the God of Wonders. I will meditate on Your Greatness! And speak of Your works! You are perfect, who is like You? I marvel at Your work. Thank you for the rain, it cleans the air and gives us a chance to start afresh." (Repeat three times)

**Contemplatio:** Reread everything once
(Pause at least 30 seconds to consider deeper meanings)

Write what you're thinking, anything, no matter what it is, write your thought in the space below:

It is a day of rest, so try to relax in knowing God is so Great we have no words to explain Him!

# CHRIST IN THE DYING MOMENT
## WEEK SIX

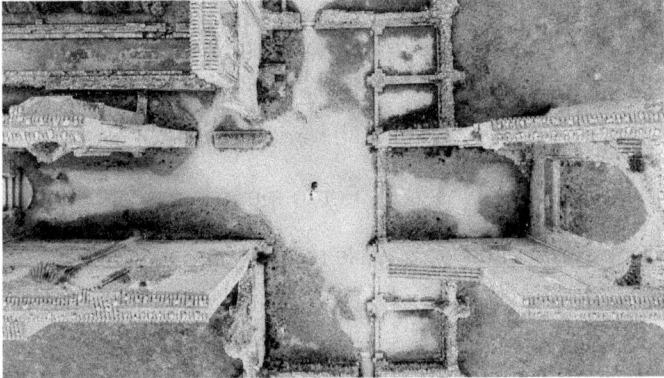

SweetIceCream Photography - Rivedoux-Plage, France

Sometimes the only way out of darkness is to let the thing that is hurting you die. That is not easy. And most of the time you have to kill it. Choke it off, or most often, just stop feeding it. But how? That is the catch, like almost everything in life the solution is simple to say, but not easy to do.

That is where forcing yourself outside is important, forcing yourself to move on is important, every time your mind wants to go back and dwell on it you must force yourself past it.

As the saying goes you must die to yourself, to live in Christ.

So, how do you deal with the darkness? Kill it. Be brutal with it, but reach out to Jesus.

**And hold onto Jesus in the Dying Moment!**

## WEEK SIX | DAY ONE

**Lectio:** "The Cedar tree is a wonderful type of the Christian. It grows by dying. As it develops, stately and beautiful, putting forth new boughs and leaves, the old ones drop off to give strength to the new ones. Likewise, the Saints live to die and die to live.
-- Vernon Hart
(Think about each word while rereading)

**Scriptio:** Philippians 1:21 "For to me to live is Christ, and to die is gain"
(Think about each word while rereading)

**Meditatio:** Reread everything
(Pause for at least 30 seconds to absorb everything)

**Oratio:** "Jesus give me the courage to face this moment head on, not fearing for my own comforts, but caring only to stay close to You. You Love me even when I am in doubt.  Please save me from myself."
(Repeat three times)

**Contemplatio:** Reread everything once
(Pause at least 30 seconds to consider deeper meanings)

What are you thinking?

Write what you're thinking, anything, no matter what it is, write your thought in the space below:

Now go on with your day!

## WEEK SIX | DAY TWO

**Lectio:** "The Cedar tree is a wonderful type of the Christian. It grows by dying. As it develops, stately and beautiful, putting forth new boughs and leaves, the old ones drop off to give strength to the new ones. Likewise, the Saints live to die and die to live.
-- Vernon Hart
(Think about each word while rereading)

**Scriptio:** Philippians 1:22-23 "But if I live in the flesh, this is the fruit of my labor: yet what I shall choose I know not. For I am in a strait between two, having a desire to depart, and to be with Christ; which is far better:"
(Think about each word while rereading)

**Meditatio:** Reread everything
(Pause for at least 30 seconds to absorb everything)

**Oratio:** "Holy Spirit speak to my soul. Help me to stay committed to Your plan. I want so badly for it to just end and be in Heaven with You. Soothe my soul and teach me to die to myself and live for You."
(Repeat three times)

**Contemplatio:** Reread everything once
(Pause at least 30 seconds to consider deeper meanings)

What are you thinking?

Write what you're thinking, anything, no matter what it is, write your thought in the space below:

Now go on with your day!

## WEEK SIX | DAY THREE

**Lectio:** "The Cedar tree is a wonderful type of the Christian. It grows by dying. As it develops, stately and beautiful, putting forth new boughs and leaves, the old ones drop off to give strength to the new ones. Likewise, the Saints live to die and die to live.
-- Vernon Hart
(Think about each word while rereading)

**Scriptio:** Philippians 1:24-25 "Nevertheless to abide in the flesh is more necessary for you. And having this confidence, I know that I shall abide and continue with you all for your furtherance and joy of faith;"
(Think about each word while rereading)

**Meditatio:** Reread everything
(Pause for at least 30 seconds to absorb everything)

**Oratio:** "Jesus teach me to enjoy the struggle. Teach me to find pleasure in Your people. Continue to work on me, that I may find peace knowing Your work is being done. Give me joy of Faith."
(Repeat three times)

**Contemplatio:** Reread everything once
(Pause at least 30 seconds to consider deeper meanings)

What are you thinking?

Write what you're thinking, anything, no matter what it is, write your thought in the space below:

Now go on with your day!

## WEEK SIX | DAY FOUR

**Lectio:** "The Cedar tree is a wonderful type of the Christian. It grows by dying. As it develops, stately and beautiful, putting forth new boughs and leaves, the old ones drop off to give strength to the new ones. Likewise, the Saints live to die and die to live.
-- Vernon Hart
(Think about each word while rereading)

**Scriptio:** Philippians 1:26 "That your rejoicing may be more abundant in Jesus Christ for me by my coming to you again."
(Think about each word while rereading)

**Meditatio:** Reread everything
(Pause for at least 30 seconds to absorb everything)

**Oratio:** "Holy Spirit continue to give me a renewed joy in reading the Bible. Help me to not grow stagnant. Help me to overflow with the love of Christ and be a constant reminder of God's love for everyone, always. and forever."
(Repeat three times)

**Contemplatio:** Reread everything once
(Pause at least 30 seconds to consider deeper meanings)

What are you thinking?

Write what you're thinking, anything, no matter what it is, write your thought in the space below:

Now go on with your day!

## WEEK SIX | DAY FIVE

**Lectio:** "The Cedar tree is a wonderful type of the Christian. It grows by dying. As it develops, stately and beautiful, putting forth new boughs and leaves, the old ones drop off to give strength to the new ones. Likewise, the Saints live to die and die to live.
-- Vernon Hart
(Think about each word while rereading)

**Scriptio:** Philippians 1:27 "Only let your conversation be as it becomes the gospel of Christ: that whether I come and see you, or else be absent, I may hear of your affairs, that all of you stand fast in one spirit, with one mind striving together for the faith of the gospel;"
(Think about each word while rereading)

**Meditatio:** Reread everything
(Pause for at least 30 seconds to absorb everything)

**Oratio:** "Jesus keep Your Gospel always on my lips. Help me to be willing to serve others and give me the ability to yield when needed. Teach me to not follow my own will, but Your will always."
(Repeat three times)

**Contemplatio:** Reread everything once
(Pause at least 30 seconds to consider deeper meanings)

What are you thinking?

Write what you're thinking, anything, no matter what it is, write your thought in the space below:

Now go on with your day!

## WEEK SIX | DAY SIX

**Lectio:** "The Cedar tree is a wonderful type of the Christian. It grows by dying. As it develops, stately and beautiful, putting forth new boughs and leaves, the old ones drop off to give strength to the new ones. Likewise, the Saints live to die and die to live.
-- Vernon Hart
(Think about each word while rereading)

**Scriptio:** Philippians 1:28 "And in nothing terrified by your adversaries: which is to them an evident token of perdition, but to you of salvation, and that of God."
(Think about each word while rereading)

**Meditatio:** Reread everything
(Pause for at least 30 seconds to absorb everything)

**Oratio:** "Jesus teach me to control my emotions. Work on me from the inside out. So that even if I am hated, I will show Your endless love. Fill my soul with your calming presence."
(Repeat three times)

**Contemplatio:** Reread everything once
(Pause at least 30 seconds to consider deeper meanings)

What are you thinking?

Write what you're thinking, anything, no matter what it is, write your thought in the space below:

Now go on with your day!

## WEEK SIX | DAY SEVEN

**Lectio:** "The Cedar tree is a wonderful type of the Christian. It grows by dying. As it develops, stately and beautiful, putting forth new boughs and leaves, the old ones drop off to give strength to the new ones. Likewise, the Saints live to die and die to live.
-- Vernon Hart
(Think about each word while rereading)

**Scriptio:** Philippians 1:29 "For unto you it is given on the behalf of Christ, not only to believe on him, but also to suffer for his sake;"
(Think about each word while rereading)

**Meditatio:** Reread everything
(Pause for at least 30 seconds to absorb everything)

**Oratio:** "Lord Jesus, may I always be for you, as you are for me. Help me to seek You in everything. In every struggle, in every moment of doubt, in every instance where I can't find it inside myself to follow Your call, take my hand. Drag me if you must. Be the one and only purpose of my life. Empty me till all that is left is You! Only You Jesus! Make me so that You are all I see! Help me endure. Help me live for You!"
(Repeat three times)

**Contemplatio:** Reread everything once
(Pause at least 30 seconds to consider deeper meanings)

Write what you're thinking, anything, no matter what it is, write your thought in the space below:

It is the seventh day, a day of rest, so try to relax in knowing Jesus Cares deeply for you!

# CHRIST IN THE HOPELESSNESS
## WEEK SEVEN

Jenny Caywood - Brown house covered with snow

There are times when you think you are out of the woods, you can see the light beyond the darkness, and then suddenly something happens, you just wake up one day and it is all meaningless. But it doesn't need to be an event, it can just be that your mind just will not shut up. And it turns to existential dread.

That is the trap of depression. But if you just keep striving, fighting for the Light, you can pull through. But you're allowed to feel various emotions. You're allowed to be vulnerable.

**Maybe you just need to take a break, and give yourself permission to rest for a while.**

## WEEK SEVEN | DAY ONE

**Lectio:** When Pope Pius V was dying, he cried out despairingly: "When I was in a low condition, I had some hopes of salvation; when I was advanced to be a cardinal, I greatly doubted it; but since I came to the popedom I have no hope at all."
(Think about each word while rereading)

**Scriptio**: Romans 7:15-16 "For that which I work, I understand not. for what I want, that do I not; but what I hate, that I do. If then I do that which I want not, I prove the law [of God], that it is good."
(Think about each word while rereading)

**Meditatio:** Reread everything
(Pause for at least 30 seconds to absorb everything)

**Oratio:** "Jesus I am disgusted with myself. Please forgive me. For what I want, that do I not; but what I hate, that I do. For me and the hardest thing is what I should. Please work your Law in me that I may bring glory and honor to You my savior."
(Repeat three times)

**Contemplatio:** Reread everything once
(Pause at least 30 seconds to consider deeper meanings)

What are you thinking?

Write what you're thinking, anything, no matter what it is, write your thought in the space below:

Now go on with your day!

## WEEK SEVEN | DAY TWO

**Lectio:** When Pope Pius V was dying, he cried out despairingly: "When I was in a low condition, I had some hopes of salvation; when I was advanced to be a cardinal, I greatly doubted it; but since I came to the popedom I have no hope at all."
(Think about each word while rereading)

**Scriptio**: Romans 7:17-18 "Now then it is no more I that do it, but sin that dwells in me. For I know that in me (that is, in my flesh,) dwells no good thing: for to want is present with me; but how to perform that which is good I find not."
(Think about each word while rereading)

**Meditatio:** Reread everything
(Pause for at least 30 seconds to absorb everything)

**Oratio:** "Jesus, You are enough. You are all anyone needs. In me dwells no good thing. The desire is present but I cannot perform it. Be with me. Hold me close because right now I feel like I can't hold on any more."
(Repeat three times)

**Contemplatio:** Reread everything once
(Pause at least 30 seconds to consider deeper meanings)

What are you thinking?

Write what you're thinking, anything, no matter what it is, write your thought in the space below:

Now go on with your day!

## WEEK SEVEN | DAY THREE

**Lectio:** When Pope Pius V was dying, he cried out despairingly: "When I was in a low condition, I had some hopes of salvation; when I was advanced to be a cardinal, I greatly doubted it; but since I came to the popedom I have no hope at all."
(Think about each word while rereading)

**Scriptio**: Romans 7:19 "For the good that I want I do not: but the evil which I want not, that I do."
(Think about each word while rereading)

**Meditatio:** Reread everything
(Pause for at least 30 seconds to absorb everything)

**Oratio:** "Jesus How can You like me when I don't like myself. Father how can you love me when I don't love myself. The good I want I do not. But the evil I hate I do. My heart is darkness. My soul is black. I am disgusted by my doubts and my sinful nature. Stay close."
(Repeat three times)

**Contemplatio:** Reread everything once
(Pause at least 30 seconds to consider deeper meanings)

What are you thinking?

Write what you're thinking, anything, no matter what it is, write your thought in the space below:

Now go on with your day!

## WEEK SEVEN | DAY FOUR

**Lectio:** When Pope Pius V was dying, he cried out despairingly: "When I was in a low condition, I had some hopes of salvation; when I was advanced to be a cardinal, I greatly doubted it; but since I came to the popedom I have no hope at all."
(Think about each word while rereading)

**Scriptio**: Romans 7:20 "Now if I do that I would not, it is no more I that do it, but sin that dwells in me"
(Think about each word while rereading)

**Meditatio:** Reread everything
(Pause for at least 30 seconds to absorb everything)

**Oratio:** "I know that I do what is evil. But I am sinful by nature. Sin dwells in my body and mind. Holy Spirit work on me. Cleanse this dark heart. Kill the body if need be, but save my soul. Keep me in your peace, that one day I may sit on the shores of Heaven. I may only be a pauper without a crown in Heaven. But I'll take it, just to be close to you Jesus."
(Repeat three times)

**Contemplatio:** Reread everything once
(Pause at least 30 seconds to consider deeper meanings)

What are you thinking?

Write what you're thinking, anything, no matter what it is, write your thought in the space below:

Now go on with your day!

## WEEK SEVEN | DAY FIVE

**Lectio:** When Pope Pius V was dying, he cried out despairingly: "When I was in a low condition, I had some hopes of salvation; when I was advanced to be a cardinal, I greatly doubted it; but since I came to the popedom I have no hope at all."
(Think about each word while rereading)

**Scriptio**: Romans 7:21-22 "I find then a law, that, when I would do good, evil is present with me. For I delight in the law of God after the inward man:"
(Think about each word while rereading)

**Meditatio:** Reread everything
(Pause for at least 30 seconds to absorb everything)

**Oratio:** "Why would you make me knowing I'd be like this? Why would you create such a worthless wretch! Even when I do good evil is still present within me. I love You in my heart, but my desire for sin overwhelms me. Why do I, the clay, rage at the potter? What place is it of mine to tell you what to do in your creation? But why would you make such a worthless man? Is it to prove you can make anything into a masterpiece? Yes! I rest in this, that You can make even me worth saving! Make me more like You!"
(Repeat three times)

**Contemplatio:** Reread everything once
(Pause at least 30 seconds to consider deeper meanings)

What are you thinking?

Write what you're thinking, anything, no matter what it is, write your thought in the space below:

Now go on with your day!

## WEEK SEVEN | DAY SIX

**Lectio:** When Pope Pius V was dying, he cried out despairingly: "When I was in a low condition, I had some hopes of salvation; when I was advanced to be a cardinal, I greatly doubted it; but since I came to the popedom I have no hope at all."
(Think about each word while rereading)

**Scriptio**: Romans 7:23 "But I see another law in my members, warring against the law of my mind, and bringing me into captivity to the law of sin which is in my members."
(Think about each word while rereading)

**Meditatio:** Reread everything
(Pause for at least 30 seconds to absorb everything)

**Oratio:** "I'm losing this battle. I see the law You put in my body, that when You enter a war happens against my mind. Because I am evil, and the only way for You to fix me, is to first kill the evil in me. You have called me out. You have saved me. Now I ask you to sanctify me. Make me into something worthy of the title Child of God. You have been here from the beginning. You can do anything, even change a worthless man like me. Thank you for what you will do."
(Repeat three times)

**Contemplatio:** Reread everything once
(Pause at least 30 seconds to consider deeper meanings)

What are you thinking?

Write what you're thinking, anything, no matter what it is, write your thought in the space below:

Now go on with your day!

## WEEK SEVEN | DAY SEVEN

**Lectio:** When Pope Pius V was dying, he cried out despairingly: "When I was in a low condition, I had some hopes of salvation; when I was advanced to be a cardinal, I greatly doubted it; but since I came to the popedom I have no hope at all."
(Think about each word while rereading)

**Scriptio**: Romans 7:24-25 "O wretched man that I am! who shall deliver me from the body of this death? I thank God it's Jesus Christ our Lord. So then with the mind I myself serve the law of God; but with the flesh the law of sin."
(Think about each word while rereading)

**Meditatio:** Reread everything
(Pause for at least 30 seconds to absorb everything)

**Oratio:** "Deliver me from this body of death. I am an incomplete work. I have been broken beyond man's ability to repair. I have so many cracks. Shine on me. You're your Light will shine through my cracks and others may see that anything is possible, even in me. Make the darkness recoil. Be near, live in me, through me; use me for Your glory. Set me on the Rock that I might be firm in my faith. Forgive my doubt. Today is a new day to get it right. Today is another chance to live for You."
(Repeat three times)

**Contemplatio:** Reread everything once
(Pause at least 30 seconds to consider deeper meanings)

Write what you're thinking, anything, no matter what it is, write your thought in the space below:


It is the seventh day, a day of rest, so try to relax in knowing Jesus WANTS To Be With You so much He gave His own life!

# Christ in the Rebuild
## WEEK EIGHT

Samuel Scrimshaw

Get up and go!

I know you hurt, your body hurts, your head hurts and it feels like you are in a fog, believe it or not moving will make that go away! You rested, now go and do something, anything, take a trip through a forest, go to a park, read a newspaper at a shopping center, get a coffee at a McDonald's and watch the people around you. Go BUILD something. The reason why it feels like no one cares is because you have removed yourself from life. It's not that they don't care, in fact, likely they bugged you incessantly when you first stopped taking part in life. They didn't stop caring, they just got used to how you are, just like when you were the sad mopey one, they got used to that. But you need to build yourself back up, and the best way to do that is to build something else, I'm using build as a catch-all for make, create, anything that is contribution to the world. Painting, sawing, writing poems or blogs, review movies online, meet with a bible study group, go to church, read the bible, go to the library and ask what events they are doing, watch someone's kid for an hour while they go to the doctor or a store.

It is time to start being. What makes us special is that we have the image of God, and that means intent, God intended to make this world, He intended for you to exist. It is time to be intentional in how you contribute to the world. Proverbs says Wisdom builds a house, with an 's', meaning continually.

**So GO!**
**The Holy Spirit will go with you, It is time to rebuild your life, Jesus has you covered on the hammer and nails.**

## WEEK EIGHT | DAY ONE

**Lectio:** At a meeting of the Fellowship of Christian Athletes, Bobby Richardson, former New York Yankee second baseman, offered a prayer that is a classic in brevity and poignancy: "Dear God, Your will. Nothing more, nothing less, nothing else. Amen."
-- Biblical Recorder
(Think about each word while rereading)

**Scriptio:** Proverbs 8:1 "Does not wisdom cry? and understanding put forth her voice?"
(Think about each word while rereading)

**Meditatio:** Reread everything
(Pause for at least 30 seconds to absorb everything)

**Oratio:** "Jesus with great wisdom comes great despair. Jesus hold me as I cry, give me understanding so that I can see Your will through my tears. Double my resolve. Give me faith, for I am faithless at times. Send me forth and give me courage. Teach me peace. Guide me in wisdom. Help me not to bruise any more of your children."
(Repeat three times)

**Contemplatio:** Reread everything once
(Pause at least 30 seconds to consider deeper meanings)

What are you thinking?

Write what you're thinking, anything, no matter what it is, write your thought in the space below:

Now go on with your day!

## WEEK EIGHT | DAY TWO

**Lectio:** At a meeting of the Fellowship of Christian Athletes, Bobby Richardson, former New York Yankee second baseman, offered a prayer that is a classic in brevity and poignancy: "Dear God, Your will. Nothing more, nothing less, nothing else. Amen."
-- Biblical Recorder
(Think about each word while rereading)

**Scriptio:** Proverbs 8:2 "She stands in the top of high places, by the way in the places of the paths."
(Think about each word while rereading)

**Meditatio:** Reread everything
(Pause for at least 30 seconds to absorb everything)

**Oratio:** "Jesus give me the courage to stand strong for You. Give me courage to climb to the mountain top, that I can stand on your High Places. Guide me by the way, keep me on road. Guide me by the way, through the rough patches of the path. I will go where you send me. Protect me on my path and calm my restless heart."
(Repeat three times)

**Contemplatio:** Reread everything once
(Pause at least 30 seconds to consider deeper meanings)

What are you thinking?

Write what you're thinking, anything, no matter what it is, write your thought in the space below:

Now go on with your day!

## WEEK EIGHT | DAY THREE

**Lectio:** At a meeting of the Fellowship of Christian Athletes, Bobby Richardson, former New York Yankee second baseman, offered a prayer that is a classic in brevity and poignancy: "Dear God, Your will. Nothing more, nothing less, nothing else. Amen."
-- Biblical Recorder
(Think about each word while rereading)

**Scriptio:** Proverbs 8:3-5 "She cries at the gates, at the entry of the city, at the coming in at the doors. Unto you, O men, I call; and my voice is to the sons of man. O all of you simple, understand wisdom: and, all of you fools, be all of you of an understanding heart."
(Think about each word while rereading)

**Meditatio:** Reread everything
(Pause for at least 30 seconds to absorb everything)

**Oratio:** "Hear my cries O Lord! Give me a voice that calls out to the people of my city. Give me the words to say that all simple will understand Your wisdom. That the unbelieving will see The Truth. That all those who mock and scorn, who hate and yell, who cry and were hurt by the church will understand in their heart that it is You, and You alone who brings wisdom and peace."
(Repeat three times)

**Contemplatio:** Reread everything once
(Pause at least 30 seconds to consider deeper meanings)

What are you thinking? Write it in the space below:

Now go on with your day!

## WEEK EIGHT | DAY FOUR

**Lectio:** At a meeting of the Fellowship of Christian Athletes, Bobby Richardson, former New York Yankee second baseman, offered a prayer that is a classic in brevity and poignancy: "Dear God, Your will. Nothing more, nothing less, nothing else. Amen."
-- Biblical Recorder
(Think about each word while rereading)

**Scriptio:** Proverbs 8:6 "Hear; for I will speak of excellent things; and the opening of my lips shall be right things."
(Think about each word while rereading)

**Meditatio:** Reread everything
(Pause for at least 30 seconds to absorb everything)

**Oratio:** "Holy Spirit give me the words! Make my speech be what You desire. Bring forth the passion to want to be your mouthpiece. I have lost the desire to speak for You. Give me grace that I may speak excellent things. That all that comes from my lips will be right things. Correct me tongue that I may be a clean vessel for you.
(Repeat three times)

**Contemplatio:** Reread everything once
(Pause at least 30 seconds to consider deeper meanings)

What are you thinking?

Write what you're thinking, anything, no matter what it is, write your thought in the space below:

Now go on with your day!

## WEEK EIGHT | DAY FIVE

**Lectio:** At a meeting of the Fellowship of Christian Athletes, Bobby Richardson, former New York Yankee second baseman, offered a prayer that is a classic in brevity and poignancy: "Dear God, Your will. Nothing more, nothing less, nothing else. Amen."
-- Biblical Recorder
(Think about each word while rereading)

**Scriptio:** Proverbs 8:7-8 "For my mouth shall speak truth; and wickedness is an abomination to my lips. All the words of my mouth are in righteousness; there is nothing perverse or perverse in them."
(Think about each word while rereading)

**Meditatio:** Reread everything
(Pause for at least 30 seconds to absorb everything)

**Oratio:** "Holy Spirit renew my mind that all of my speech will be only truth continually. Make me despise the things You despise. Make all the words I speak be things of righteousness. Renew my resolve and let nothing perverse come from my mouth."
(Repeat three times)

**Contemplatio:** Reread everything once
(Pause at least 30 seconds to consider deeper meanings)

What are you thinking?

Write what you're thinking, anything, no matter what it is, write your thought in the space below:

Now go on with your day

## WEEK EIGHT | DAY SIX

**Lectio:** At a meeting of the Fellowship of Christian Athletes, Bobby Richardson, former New York Yankee second baseman, offered a prayer that is a classic in brevity and poignancy: "Dear God, Your will. Nothing more, nothing less, nothing else. Amen."
-- Biblical Recorder
(Think about each word while rereading)

**Scriptio:** Proverbs 8:9-10 "They are all plain to him that understands, and right to them that find knowledge. Receive my instruction, and not silver; and knowledge rather than choice gold."
(Think about each word while rereading)

**Meditatio:** Reread everything
(Pause for at least 30 seconds to absorb everything)

**Oratio:** "Holy Spirit make all things plain to me, that I can understand You. Help me to understand the things that I learn and read. Guide my heart that I will receive Your instruction and value it more than silver. And make knowledge of You more precious to me than gold."
(Repeat three times)

**Contemplatio:** Reread everything once
(Pause at least 30 seconds to consider deeper meanings)

What are you thinking?

Write what you're thinking, anything, no matter what it is, write your thought in the space below:

Now go on with your day!

## WEEK EIGHT | DAY SEVEN

**Lectio:** At a meeting of the Fellowship of Christian Athletes, Bobby Richardson, former New York Yankee second baseman, Offered a prayer that is a classic in brevity and poignancy: "Dear God, Your will. Nothing more, nothing less, nothing else. Amen."
-- Biblical Recorder
(Think about each word while rereading)

**Scriptio:** Proverbs 8:11-13 "For wisdom is better than rubies; and all the things that may be desired are not to be compared to it. I wisdom dwell with prudence, and find out knowledge of witty inventions. The fear of the LORD is to hate evil: pride, and arrogance, and the evil way, and the perverse mouth, do I hate."
(Think about each word while rereading)

**Meditatio:** Reread everything
(Pause for at least 30 seconds to absorb everything)

**Oratio:** "Jesus, You are Wisdom! Help me to see Your worth with each passing day. Help me desire You more than any thing on this evil earth. Give me Your prudence. Give me discernment. Teach me to revere You more and to despise all evil. Guide my tongue, that You will be happy with my speech. Continue to fill me with Your wisdom!"
(Repeat three times)

**Contemplatio:** Reread everything once
(Pause at least 30 seconds to consider deeper meanings)

Write what you're thinking, anything, no matter what it is, write your thought in the space below:


It is the seventh day, a day of rest, so try to relax in knowing Jesus Died To Save Those He Loves, And He Loves You, even if you don't love Him!

# RECOMMENDED READING:

## HAVE DOUBTS?
"Mere Christianity" by C.S. Lewis
"A Grief Observed" by C. S. Lewis


## NEED THEOLOGY?
"The Potter's Promise" by Leighton Flowers
"God's Provision For All" by Leighton Flowers
"The Atonement" by David L. Allen
"The Extent of the Atonement" by David L. Allen
"What Love is This?" by Dave Hunt
"The God Makers" by Ed Decker & Dave Hunt
"Letters to a Mormon Elder" by Dr. James R. White
"The Unseen Realm" by Dr. Michael S. Heiser
"Reversing Hermon" by Dr. Michael S. Heiser
"The Second Coming of the New Age"
by Steven Bancarz & Josh Peck
"Mystery Babylon" by Chris White
"False Christ" by Chris White


## NEED SPIRITUAL-IMPROVEMENT?
"Just Jesus Them" by John Stahl
#EmojiBibleProject by John Stahl
"12 Rules for Life" by Jordan B. Peterson
"Uncommon Courage" by Tony Dungy
"True Spirituality" by Chip Ingram
"Letters to an Incarcerated Brother" by Hill Harper
"Man Up!" by Jody Burkeen
"Kingdom Man" by Tony Evans
"No More Excuses" by Tony Evans

# <u>Stay in Touch</u>

## WE'D LOVE TO HEAR FROM YOU:

TheChristianNomad.com
TheShadow.Land

## CONTACT THE CHRISTIAN NOMAD:

Twitter & Facebook @NomadChristian